Slices

of

Life

Slices of Life

Inspirations & Understandings

Susan Lannan Hicks

PRECISE COMMUNICATIONS
Waynesville, NC

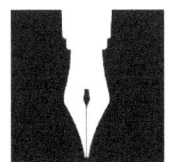

SLICES OF LIFE: INSPIRATIONS AND UNDERSTANDINGS © 2024 by Susan Lannan Hicks. All rights reserved. No part of this book may be used or reproduced in any manner whatsoever without written permission except in the case of brief quotations embodied in critical articles and reviews. For more information, contact Precise Communications, 97 Morning Drive, Waynesville, NC 28786.

1st Edition

Library of Congress Control Number: 2024913369

ISBN 978-0-999-4564-5-3 (print)

Cover Design by White Studios, Kimberly McClure

Front cover art © Joan Doyle, "North Carolina Dogwoods"
www.artistryoflife.com

Back cover art portraits and Peace Tree design © Kerra Hicks

Introduction...

I've always been a bit of a dabbler, and several times I've set out to write a book, often producing multiple chapters. I'm hoping some will see the light of day over the coming years, but this collection seemed like the best way to get some writings out sooner rather than later.

Sometimes writing comes out like a flow, thoughts and words producing writing worth keeping and sharing.

Sometimes it takes a long time to reach fruition, perhaps half written or nearly done but not completed for a long while.

The first poem I remember writing was started while I was still in high school, the first two lines coming easily. The rest was worked and rejected and reworked until it finally finished as:

> Why do willows weep?
> Why do oaks shed acorn tears?
> Could it be they see tomorrow –
> the culmination of my fears?

I lost several poems that were in my purse/satchel when I was mugged and my satchel was stolen. I didn't care about money or anything else that was stolen, but I have mourned the loss of the poems, some of which still haunt me in vague flashes of memory. One was very special to me, and I was eventually able to recreate it.

Jesus, why didn't you start a super-race
while you were here on earth?
You could have sent our genetic pool
sky high with just one birth.

Why did you roam all of your days
And never take a wife?
You could have changed our history
by co-creating a life.

Did you pass on the best of you
by sharing how you think?
You could have been more egotistical
and forged a human link.

You missed the opportunity
to meld us with your gold.
Now all that we have left of you
is some stories they say that you told.

 In context of my limited exposure at the time to spiritual beliefs and religions other than the one I was raised in, this made sense at the time. I realize there's room for discussion about many elements, but I leave that to your imagination.

The lines that stick in my brain and resurface countless times are: Did you pass on the best of you / by sharing how you think?

It resulted in this current work, to share some of how I think. I hope at least some of it resonates with you.

Thank you for reading it and for continuing to grow.

Sincerely,
Susan

Contents

Freshman Lessons 1
   1967-1968 3
   No means no, except 7
   Rules Bend, Reality Varies 10
   FROM PLAY TO A WHOLE NEW WORLD VIEW 13
   Shared Dream 18

Inspirations 21
   Start where you are 22

Poetic Musings 29
   A (Sorta) Sonnet 30
   Poetic Musings 31
   Untitled 32
   Coinsight 34

Understandings 35
   Stopping the Downward Spiral 36
   Dealing with Disappointment 38
   The evolution of my prayers 41

Inspired by Love 45
   Mission Statement 46
   You're The One 48
   Anniversary Sonnet 49

Saying No 51
   Saying "No" 52

Inspired by Love Too 57
Ode to an Adoptive Grandmother 58
Primary Love 60
Almost 2 61
Almost 2, Too 62

Listen to Your Body or It Might Get Loud 63
My Body Lessons 64
Good Changes 76

Pondering Life and Death 77
Parallel Excavations 78
Death, be not proud 80
Half-Year Reflections 82
Since Mom Died… 83
Sweet soul released 84

Reflections 85
Heart to Heart 86
Appreciate Abundance 89
Gratitude Prayers 91

Inspired 93
In Praise of Sunset Visions 94
To Oliver 95
Sea Love 96
My Brother's Poem 98

Freshman Lessons

Reading is like eating

and writing is like planting a garden.

Ideas and experiences are dug up, turned over,

chopped and probed, preparing the soil.

Sometimes additional fertilizer must be gathered

(from garden store or library stockpiles) and applied.

Seeds removed from yesterday's fruit,

properly nurtured, provide

tomorrow's nourishment.

1967-1968

In the winter of 1967-68, I was a freshman attending Duquesne University in Pittsburgh, Pennsylvania. That year, the university had accepted more students than it could house on campus, preparing for the construction of and raising cash to build more dormitories. I was among the incoming students selected to be housed at Point Part College, located approximately one mile away from the campus.

The walk through the city and up the steep hill to campus didn't really bother me, even when it rained for what seemed like (or may actually have been) 40 days in a row that Spring – I bought a pink raincoat and a black vinyl rain hat and adopted the attitude that I would not let weather bother me.

But as the fall turned into winter, the brisk and chilly winds turned bitter cold. Walking the city streets through the wind tunnels created by tall buildings, I was bothered by a rule that the university had at the time I enrolled: Female students must wear skirts while on campus (or maybe it was in all classes).

I'd been raised in a middle-class, Catholic family, and I had skirts – lined wool skirts that were popular at the time, and my mom made sure I had sweaters that coordinated with them. She also bought me some lined wool Bermuda-length shorts to match. Along with sweater tights and tall boots, the wool shorts made the walk across town much more bearable.

It made so much more sense to me, to wear wool shorts instead of a skirt that let the wind blow chilly in places that wanted to be warm. So, I did wear the shorts to class. And then so did others. They were a dressy style and were the same length as the skirts we were wearing – and I believe they often went unnoticed to the casual observer.

It was a small rebellion, not meant to confront authority but to assert my/our right to not be bound by an archaic rule, a rule that seemed to make no sense and was definitely sexist (though that term was not in my vocabulary at the time).

As time went on, campus dress codes became virtually ignored, and to my knowledge the requirement that females wear skirts on campus was no longer enforced. From wool shorts to dress slacks and on to jeans, campus attire reflected the changes arising in America. Personal preference in style, comfort and convenience grew in importance, despite society's pressure to conform to "acceptable" clothing and hair styles.

"Hair" opened on Broadway in the spring of 1968, but hair freedom had already started to grow. One example of breaking from the norm and coming out for the better was Twiggy – the British model and singer who, with extremely short hair and very thin frame, became an icon of the Mod movement in London. And that was a lucky break for me.

My hair had been in a nice, shoulder-length style, a flip it was called, in my senior year of high school, until I went to the Jersey shore with my girlfriends, probably during Spring break. Some of the girls had short hair, and I'd been talking about cutting my hair short for so long that one of them finally said, "Lannan, shut up or get the scissors."

Huh! Hah! So, scissors were found and my hair was cut by totally untrained teenagers, and it turned out a bit of a mess. Thoughts of upcoming proms and graduation apparently never occurred to me at the time, though they certainly did afterward.

I went to a hairdresser a few times later that spring, trying to get my hair and especially my hairline to look decent. It's not as though I had tons of hair – mine is on the thin and fine side, and the hairline shape was very noticeable. It was a time when hair products and tools were not nearly as available as they are these days, and managing a new style was a challenge.

Then, the thought of going to college started to grow stronger, along with the realization that I would need to try to fit into a whole new culture and group of people. When my mother asked me to take my younger brothers for their pre-school-year haircuts, I sat in the barber shop waiting for them and it occurred to me that a barber could probably trim my hairline better than a hairdresser. So, I asked him to cut my hair.

A bit startled by the unusual request (male and female grooming services had not yet overlapped), but willing, he cut my hair. Cut it like any three-year-old boy would be proud of. The back of my head had a bristle of hair about ¼ inch long, and the front hairs were maybe as long as half an inch.

I cried when I looked in the mirror at home, thinking the girls in the dorm would think I was a dyke. (My apologies to those of varying sexual preferences, much more understood and accepted today.) My salvation was that as soon as I hit campus, I was given the nickname "Twiggy" (I was very thin at the time), which gave me a bit of recognition on campus and some confidence that my appearance was "acceptable."

Having spent too much time standing with my back to a mirror and juggling a hand-held mirror, a pair of scissors and a comb – to see the back of my head and fix my hairline after hairdressers had left it a mess – and trying to save money, I started cutting my own hair in college. Walking daily across town, the wind was a force to be reckoned with, and I cut my hair so that none of it would reach my eyes, then styled it as I could. Before long, I was cutting one of my room-mate's hair, and then other girls in the dorm wing started asking me to cut their hair. No money exchanged hands, just goodwill.

My younger brothers no longer wanted barbers who resented long hair to be in charge of their looks and soon wanted me to cut their hair, too. It went well for the most part – other than when I thought I grabbed thinning shears (but turned out to be regular shears) and made a cut that was too short near Mark's left ear. That required some creative adjustments to work it out somewhat satisfactorily, and fortunately, Mark was forgiving.

African Americans started to reclaim natural hair styles, and hippies grew their hair long. These simple but quite visible marks of differentiation and unique expression were discouraged and sometimes scorned openly by the American public that craved compliance with established norms.

The veil of a "united" country was being ripped asunder by its own children, and the disturbed "forces that be" were aroused anew to squelch the call for freedom.

THAT WAS THEN, NOW...

Here are a few indicators that freedom of personal style has not stopped being an issue:

A student was suspended from his high school for wearing a natural hairstyle in 2024.

Also in 2024, the United States Marine Corps still had a requirement that females wear panty hose as a part of their dress uniform, until it was suspended that year.

∧∧∧∧∧∧∧∧∧

"Effective immediately, the wear of hosiery with skirts is optional," the Marines Corps wrote in a statement…".

Story by Nicholas Rice U.S. Marine Corps Alters Dress Code for Women, No Longer Requiring Them to Wear Pantyhose (msn.com)

March17, 2024

∧∧∧∧∧∧∧∧∧

The range of options has widened considerably, with flowing skirts and denim halter tops once only made and worn by hippies now available from major brands at retail stores across the country. African-American styles have both reached back to cultural roots and moved the hip culture forward. From Native Americans reclaiming their heritage hairstyles to men with ponytails down the back of their business suits, personal style rights are rising.

No means no, except ...

One of the lessons learned through the process of enrolling in classes at Duquesne during my freshman year was the undeniable value of patience and perseverance in being able to achieve a desired result.

Enrolling in classes was a time-consuming and often frustrating process, in a manner that is totally foreign to today's online enrollment options. We stood in lines, long lines. We looked through paper catalogs and filled out paper class enrollment request forms. And we waited in line until we reached the front and could talk to a tired, overworked, underpaid and generally unappreciated person who had little authority other than to check numbers and accept or decline your class requests. Standing in line was a chance to talk with other students, though, and you could sometimes learn a lot about a class you were considering or the professor offering it.

I learned that if I was told a class was full and I could not enroll in it, there was no sense in arguing or pleading at that time. I would enroll in what was available and then set about trying to figure out how to get into the class I actually wanted. That generally meant going to the department and/or the professor to plead my case.

Often, if the teacher realized that I was truly interested in taking that particular class from him, and not just wanting to fill a gap in my schedule or to satisfy a degree requirement, I would get an indication as to whether the class was really full or just nearly full, along with information about checking back in or re-applying for enrollment closer to or even after the first day's class. (All my teachers were male.)

I learned to listen to the advice of other students who had taken a class I was interested in, regarding the teachers giving the course. Getting opinions from a few students, if possible, would usually give me a pretty good indication of whether it would be a good class for me. Something that was attractive to others may not always appeal to me, however, or prove to be good for me. So, I learned to listen to others with discernment.

For example, in two semesters of American literature (required for my major) I fully learned to appreciate that a class that was known as "an easy A" was definitely not always the best choice for me.

There were two American lit teachers at the time, and two semesters were required for a degree in secondary education with a major in English. One was the proverbial "easy A" professor and the other was definitely not. I opted for one semester with each one. The more challenging, demanding and difficult teacher had the ability to present a wealth of information and weave it together in an engaging manner. I really enjoyed his class, though his assignments and exams were difficult. The other professor read to the class, literally, from the works of early American authors. He would read a page or two, summarize a page or two, and return to reading. Impossibly boring. Lesson learned: Being bored is not always worth the reward.

Further lessons were gained from the boring professor's class, though, which include: Do not take too much for granted, and do not depend on the past to predict the future.

This teacher would occasionally stop to make a point about the material he was reading. Take note! Whatever he said about the works covered in class, that would be sure to be on a test. It worked every time. Read over the notes a few times to learn and remember those points, and the test would be easy.

Except the final exam wasn't.

I prepared as usual and came to take the final exam ready to answer the questions I had every reason to believe would be on it. And there they were, I saw, as soon as the test was passed out to all of us sitting ready to take it.

Only, we weren't there long. Shortly after we received the exam, the class was dismissed, as a bomb threat had been received and the building had to be evacuated.

No bomb was found. It may well have been a student who did not want to take a final exam that day. But the impact of the event on a personal level was only fully realized when I went to take the re-scheduled final exam.

Because we had seen the questions on the original exam before we had to leave the classroom, the teacher had made up a totally new exam! There wasn't one question on it that had been emphasized in his lectures or in my class notes. It was a much more difficult test, and the easy A I'd hoped for wasn't to be. A B is on my transcript for that class.

Rules Bend, Reality Varies

An English composition class in my freshman year delivered another lesson in rules not always being unwavering.

At that time, Duquesne University had a rule about attendance that required failure of any class in which absences exceeded twice the number of credits the course offered. So, a three-credit course had a limit of six absences, or the class would be failed.

I was never good at getting up and going while I was in high school. I stayed up late every night studying and doing homework, as afternoons were spent in after-school activities and dinner was followed by cleaning up and washing dishes, then came phone calls with friends or long comedy routines from my older brother who recounted his day with great and hilarious expressiveness. That was when I was in ninth grade, before he graduated and joined the Marines. My parents would wake me up multiple times in the morning before I would tear myself out of bed to stumble into the bathroom, often dozing off again sitting on the toilet.

With high school as my recent example of a normal schedule, and with the notion of taking classes in the morning and working in the afternoon, I had foolishly scheduled myself for classes that began at 8 a.m., five days a week. And the English composition class was one of them, three times a week.

I liked the class. I participated in discussions and did well on tests and assignments. Arriving on time, however, was not so easy. I tried. I often rushed along city blocks, carrying heavy literature books in my backpack, but too often arrived at the door after class had started. Most days, I'd slip in as quietly as I could and take a seat. Except when I just couldn't. Maybe I had arrived later than usual, or maybe I'd come in late too many times lately, but those days I'd get to the building my class was in and just keep walking up the hill to the Student Union.

The Rathskeller in the lower floor of the Student Union was usually pretty empty at that time of day. I'd get a cup of coffee or tea and sit and read, until someone would come along to share the table and talk.

One of my roommates (I had two) had come to Duquesne as a declared philosophy major. I didn't even know what philosophy was at that time, nor did I have a clue about psychology or sociology. But Mare attracted the attention of undergraduate and graduate students with her seriousness of study and ready laugh, and I got to know some of them as well. They frequently gathered in the Rathskeller, and I found conversation with them entirely intriguing.

At the time, I had a really hard time reading philosophy and understanding it, but listening to it, I could gain much more. So, I asked questions to probe for information and to stimulate further conversation, and I often sat for hours, missing classes but gaining an education. The thoughts and ideas that were shared were so different than any I'd been exposed to in my private school, run by nuns and focused on classical education. (Four years of Latin, four of French, and scant hard or social science offerings.)

Existential phenomenology. That was a primary focus of the philosophy and psychology departments at Duquesne when I attended. This wildly different orientation was nourished by at least one grad student who had studied with Timothy Leary. As I brought a new perspective into conversations when I returned home on breaks, my father's response would be shaking his head as though he were truly bemused while saying, "I thought I was sending you to a Catholic school."

Back to the beginning of this story: I missed more than three classes that semester, but I did not fail the class.

Lesson in fatal attraction…or not fatal, but futile.

The English teacher had developed a crush on me, I later realized. It was a class I enjoyed, but I was too naïve to discern any interest in me on the part of the teacher. It wasn't until the letters started arriving from him over summer break that I realized he was attracted to me and wanted a relationship with me. It felt creepy and weird and awkward. I rebuffed his advances.

Any pain my lack of interest might have caused him I believe was probably washed away over time by awkward feelings of his own and relief from the possible complications that a relationship with me might have brought to his life and career.

I don't recall the university's absence rule being enforced in any other circumstance either, though it may have been. Given that students were beginning to question authority and the school was looking to retain all the tuition sources it could manage, the rule may have fallen away like the skirts-on-campus policy did.

FROM PLAY TO A WHOLE NEW WORLD VIEW

In my freshman year at Duquesne, I volunteered once a week at an after-school program held in the basement of a church across the street from Pittsburgh's Civic Arena, just downhill from the Hill District.

The program was meant to offer local students assistance with their homework as well as a safe place to spend the late afternoons, I'm sure. But there was not much oversight as to what we were doing, and the kids were so wound up from sitting in school all day that the last thing they wanted to do was sit down with pencils and papers. They needed exercise and play, and I called upon my friends to help provide it.

I had been hanging out with a group of guy friends, and I asked them to come and see if they could help me. They came willingly, and they loved it. The wrestling mats stored in the church basement provided a perfect arena for wrestling and playing with the kids, like my brothers did with my father on the living room floor. Everyone had a great time, though some of the young boys got pretty aggressive and needed to be calmed down once in a while. Their excitement might have been heightened and their aggression may have been strengthened by the fact that my friends were white, of various European descent, and the students had varying dark skin tones. The whole country was simmering with an undercurrent of racial tension, and the kids had likely never had much contact of this nature with white folks.

All went well until April 1968, when Martin Luther King was assassinated.

At the time of the assassination, I was attending a retreat with the Duquesne chaplain and a group of friends. We were in a farmhouse outside of Pittsburgh, enjoying a time of shared meals and spiritual celebrations that were more open to participation.

The news reported that the airports were being shutting down. I called home to check in and let my parents know I was alright. My mom wanted me to go straight to the airport and fly home, but I had only very casual clothes with me (Easter ahead) and none of the study materials I'd need over spring break.

Upon my return to the city to gather things for leaving town, it appeared as though Pittsburgh had been invaded, with soldiers on street corners and driving around in jeeps, brandishing rifles.

I wanted to see my kids, to hug them and let them know I still cared. But barricades were set up across the roads leading up to the Hill section where they lived, and I was denied all my attempts to cross the barriers. I stood on the street and sobbed.

Students at the high school I attended were white, with two exceptions and I did not know them very well. By the time I got to Duquesne, Black students were sticking tightly together at tables in the cafeteria and would not return my smiles or acknowledge any attempts I made to be friendly. It saddened me. I didn't understand at the time their need for separation.

I was really pretty unfamiliar with the whole concepts of race and ethnicity. Raised in a family that was Irish, Scottish and Welsh, I had no idea that being Irish or Italian or having any other cultural identity played any role in politics – until I took a class on "Black America and American Political Structure" at Duquesne.

My father's bringing home what he called Serbian bread, given to him by a co-worker occasionally, when I was in grade school was a real treat – and the closest I came to having a clue that there was any difference in culture. I did have a friend in high school whose family was fiercely Italian, I learned as I spent some time with them.

When I was a freshman at Duquesne, I was friends with a student named Maury. We had some great discussions and a bit of flirtation. When someone said something to me about Maury being Jewish, I replied that he wasn't Jewish. The other person actually laughed as they corrected me, saying "With a name like Maury Schiowitz?" And when I thought of his first and last names together, I realized they were probably right. I'd gone to Catholic schools all my life, and I had not known anyone who was Jewish personally. We had Jewish neighbors, after my family moved the summer before I left for college. As my younger brothers grew up, they were much better acquainted with people of various faiths and cultures.

I took a class in Afro-American literature in the first part of my senior year at Duquesne, and I enjoyed learning about the literature with viewpoints vastly different than what I'd previously been presented with in my education. I found the rhythms of African American poetry engaging, and the seriousness of the messages in the poetry, fiction and essays we studied helped expand my understanding of human experience.

The class included an assignment to recite a work by an African American author or poet. I chose a short, rhythmic poem by Langston Hughes and practiced it as I walked back and forth to campus, letting the rhythm of my steps reinforce the meter of the poem. Though very nervous about performing it, as the instructor was a rather serious man who could be sharply critical, it went well and was one of the few recitations that was applauded by my classmates. I enjoyed working that assignment, learning and feeling the rhythm of the poem.

Racial inequity became obvious to me during that period of my life. One terrible example was that the historically Black district called the Hill District was being torn down, to be replaced with more modern, hence less affordable, structures. The community was being destroyed and displaced. Meanwhile, Black people were excluded from construction employment, so they watched as white folks tore down their homes, with no ability to benefit from the process of destruction and replacement, euphemistically called "Gentrification."

There was a protest march in the city. I remember vividly the passion and leadership of Nate Smith, who inspired me to march with him to support the challenge to the racism that excluded African Americans from work opportunities.

Also, during that period, racism seemed to justify the war in Vietnam for many people, but it did not matter to me that those we were killing and whose homeland we were destroying were any different than the people I lived among.

People were people and deserved to be treated fairly and with respect. That seemed to be the message delivered in Bible stories. I had learned of the kindness of Jesus towards those who were scorned by others. But I began to realize that the world operated on different principles than those that seemed fair to me.

The vision of army jeeps rolling through the streets of Pittsburgh, with rifles brandished to raise fear among American citizens, has never left me. Nor has the profound sadness of the loss of a leader who exemplified love and urged us to create a more peaceful and just life for all.

I returned home for the summer ready for working part-time and taking a class at Harrisburg Area Community College, along with some well needed rest and home-cooked meals.

My family had moved from outside Philadelphia to Harrisburg the summer before I started Duquesne, so there was not much invitation for or attraction to socializing with old friends. They were all 100 miles away, and high school seemed like a lifetime ago.

Vietnam was increasingly in the news, and a growing awareness of the war and its violence was magnified by the fact that my brother Rick was a Marine stationed in Vietnam. He had enlisted after graduating from high school, when the public was largely unaware of the growing foreign military involvement. Rick wasn't interested in going to college, but he wanted to make my dad proud, so he enlisted in the Marines. My mother had not been happy about his enlisting, and as the war intensified, so did her mother's anguish.

That year held one more shock.

On June 6, 1968, Robert F. Kennedy, presidential candidate who spoke of unity and justice and peace, was assassinated.

My heart broke, along with hope.

In July 1968, my brother Rick wrote from Vietnam a letter starkly describing the army's lack of support from local people and the military's ridiculous decisions, costing hundreds of lives to take an area only to abandon it soon afterward. My cousin Scott was also a Marine serving in Vietnam, and his letters conveyed the misery and hardships of fighting a jungle war.

I entered Duquesne in 1967 as a naïve freshman, steeped in the tradition of American superiority and the stability of Catholic faith. By the time I returned to Duquesne for my second year of college, life seemed very different than it had a year ago.

Shared Dream

Martin, you and I have a dream.
It only makes sense, it would seem.
We're all one and the same,
Every color and name,
We're all part of a rainbow scheme.

As we celebrate the birth of the man
Who declared that "together, we can,"
We pause to recall the wonder of all
As we marched through this land, hand in hand.

Martin, you and I have a dream.
It only makes sense, it would seem.
But when I hear the news
I start cryin' the blues
It hurts me so bad I could scream.

Yes, we still have such a long way to go
To believe in that dream, and help make it grow.
Each day as we work and meet and play,
We're one step closer or further away.
Oh, how I wish you were still here today

To help us see clearly and show us the way

Your spirit we honor, remembering your pleas

To join hands together, seeking justice and peace.

Martin, you and I have a dream

Just as clear as a sunlight beam.

And if I do my part

I know in my heart

We shall be released and redeemed.

(Song)

Written on Martin Luther King's Birthday

1988

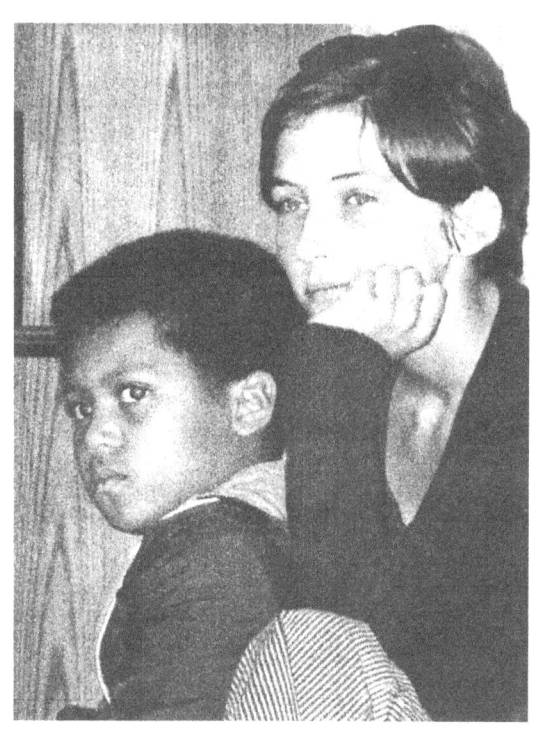
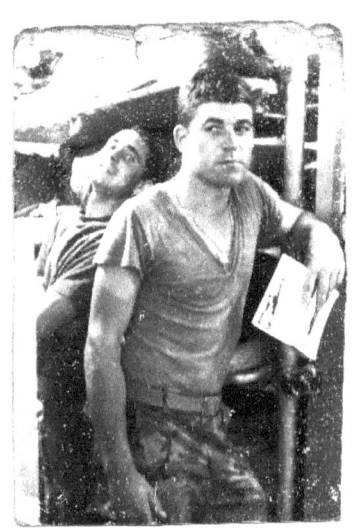

Inspirations

Start where you are

My mother grew up city poor and my father grew up country poor. They both lived through the Great Depression in the 1930s.

Together they created a lovely and welcoming home, doing much of the work themselves. They saved and when they could, they bought good furnishings and appliances, stuff that lasts.

Mom's parents had emigrated to Toronto from Scotland, young newlyweds following in the footsteps of her older sister and her husband. My youngest brother, the genealogist in the family, discovered that Grandma Doak was pregnant at the time she traveled across the Atlantic Ocean – and at the time of her marriage.

Grandma was the youngest of 9 children, and I'm sure there was plenty of social and familial pressure to relocate as well as the desire to start somewhere new, where a fudged wedding date on a document might not be as noticed.

She found plenty of sorrow and strife in the new world, though. Pop Doak was not nearly as successful as her brother-in-law had been, and the difference in social class was difficult. He also drank heavily until after returning from World War II, which made employment erratic and home life unpredictable and often uncomfortable. Mom said she never invited friends to her house.

During the war, Grandma worked in a factory. She also had four children to parent, house and feed. She managed to take them camping in the summer, though, and that created a setting for an early manifestation of the qualities that ultimately earned my mom the nickname "Clean Jean."

Mom wore white shorts, white tops and white sneakers – while camping!

She also developed pneumonia pleurisy in both lungs at the age of 16 and spent many months in a sanitorium north of the city. It was the time when they left the windows open at night, summer or winter, for fresh air to clear out the lungs. It was also the time when they had recently discovered sulfa drugs, which saved my mother's life.

When she left the hospital, money was scarce and work was readily available, with so many men away at war and women working in munitions plants – like Grandma did. Mom went to work in an office, instead of returning to school. The nice clothes she bought herself to wear to work were sometimes stretched out by her younger sister, Helen, "borrowing" them to wear to school.

Mom enjoyed a good time, and she and her girlfriends went dancing or roller skating several times a week. They also rented a cottage on Toronto Island during the summer months, which meant traveling back and forth to work in the city on a ferry. It was there she met my dad.

My father was born in Pittsford, a small town outside Rochester, New York. When his father died, my dad was barely 2 years old.

Although his father's family owned several properties and the local hotel, they apparently did not support their son's widow and young son. Grandma found work at a farm down the way, exchanging labor in the kitchen and helping with family chores for their room and board. The farmer's wife had died, leaving him with several children to raise. Grandma and the farmer eventually married, and they had a few more children together.

But Dad was the youngest for a while, and the older boys in the family were farm-raised tough and considered him a city boy, a mama's boy. My Aunt Anne, dad's half-sister, once told me that the older boys were tough on him, as was his step-father.

Greed drove the family off the farm, though, as they lost it to what was called a "demand mortgage." Money would be leant to buy a property, but the loaner could ask for full payment at any time, and if not received, the property would be reclaimed and repossessed. Charles McEneany had such a mortgage, and all was fine until the loaner died and his heir came with a full-payment demand, which could not be met. The family had to move into town.

My dad's strength was intellectual, and his interest in engineering was innate. He built his first radio using alligator clips, wire and gathered items, with his bed springs serving as an antenna. He graduated from high school early and went on to attend Rochester Institute of Technology. He worked three jobs while studying but had little money to spare, often relating that a quart of ice cream was the cheapest lunch he could buy that would satisfy his hunger.

Dad was working in radio before his World War II enlistment in the military. He worked with the U.S. Army Signal Corps and was loaned to the Royal Air Force to help set up the radar systems to warn and protect England from German bombing raids. He was sitting with other officers in New Jersey, awaiting transport to England, when the United States declared war against Germany and became an official ally of Great Britain. After serving in England, he was stationed in Toronto, Canada, training members of the Royal Air Force on how to operate and utilize radar for military defense.

Dad had been staying at the Royal York Hotel, but he rented an apartment to live on Toronto Island for the summer, which is where he met my mom.

A young American officer with a steady income and not much cooking experience, he arranged with the girls next door to help pay for groceries if they would cook and let him share meals with them. Win-win, and dad got to know some local lasses, including the one who caught his eye and heart.

When my mom agreed to marry him, she was hesitant to introduce him to her parents, uncertain of how Pop Doak would react. She made dad wait at the corner while she went in to break the news, saying she would signal him if it was okay for him to come into the house. After all, he was a Yankee, a soldier (with a future certain to take her away from her home town), four years older than her (18 and 22 years old) and a Catholic!

After Pop met my dad, he told my mom that dad reminded him of Johnny Haylock, a nephew who had been killed in the war. My mom knew it was going to be alright, as Pop had been very fond of Johnny.

Mom wanted a nice wedding, and Pop was still drinking at the time she got engaged. She told him that if he was going to take a drink at their wedding reception, he could just stay home. He was sober for their wedding, and from that point forward in his life he stopped drinking and started succeeding, eventually developing a real estate business in the lake country north of Toronto.

Shortly after they married, mom and dad moved to Asbury Park, New Jersey, to the first of many homes they would share over the years. Mom was excited to be near the ocean, and dad had to keep her away from the shore when she wanted to go there to watch an incoming storm that they later saw had moved multiple seaside boardwalk sections several blocks inland.

One incident from that period in their lives exemplified how, despite my father's status as an officer, social and cultural barriers could literally slam the door in their faces. There was an event at the Officer's Club that called for formal attire; my father wore his dress uniform, and my mother wore her best dress – a beautiful blue velvet dress she had worn when they got married. But it was a short dress – the war was on and good cloth was very expensive. They were informed at the door that the formal dress code for officers' wives required that women wear long gowns, and my mom and dad were refused entry to the event. I can only imagine how their excitement and anticipation would have crashed into disappointment and humiliation. My father never set foot in that Officer's Club again.

Mom was a knitter and a sewer. She made curtains and bedspreads and baby clothes, and she kept an immaculate home. She sewed pretty dresses for me and sometimes she made matching outfits for my doll.

My dad worked hard at home as well as in full-time employment. They dug up the earth and made a good-sized garden when I was young. They managed their money well, raising four children and doing volunteer work to benefit school and church organizations. They were kind to our friends and kept family ties as closely as they could – with mom writing weekly letters to both grandmas to share news about growing grandchildren. And my dad sent a modest check monthly to his mom to help her with expenses.

Grandma still lived in a house in Fishers, New York, with no indoor toilet facilities. It was my favorite place to visit. There was a mill pond behind her house that we swam in, sheep to chase, and railroad tracks to walk along and explore.

My husband's favorite place was his grandmother's house in Alabama, with no indoor facilities. Tom' family drove to Alabama every summer from their home in San Diego, with four kids in a station wagon (without air conditioning), camping along the way.

Tom and I started our life together living in southeast Oklahoma, in a cabin with no electricity or running water – until we made those improvements. We started where we were, used what we had, and did what we could. We saved and bought good stuff, just like we had learned from our families.

Tom's parents had bought a piece of land outside San Diego and a bulldozer while he was still in middle school, and Tom helped build the family's new home from the ground up. There's not much he isn't willing to try and able to do.

Our culture has turned into a consumer-based society, with "buy it" rather than "create it" the growing trend. It has diminished our sense of independence, and self-reliance is no longer seen as a virtue. Rather than an increased sense of community, however, we have become more self-absorbed and isolated, more reliant on commercial and industrial solutions. Entertainment, food and medicine all have huge industrial organizations producing consumables at an alarming rate.

Fortunately, there are communities where older values still prevail, helping each other and treating others with respect, and making rather than buying, creating a simpler life. Some of us make the choice to live in, participate in and cherish this type of community – which may be a network of friends, rather than defined by a geographic area. It can be developed, if you:

Start where you are.

Use what you have.

Do what you can.

Arthur Ashe

Patrick Edward Lannan, Sr.
1st Lieutenant, U.S. Army
Jean Catherine (Evans) Doak
October 16, 1943

Poetic Musings

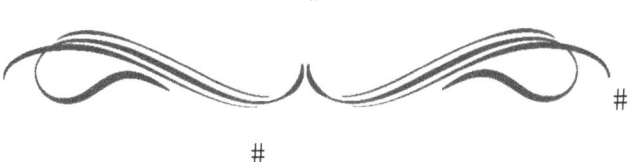

People think poets are quite mad, I know,
for caring where commas and hyphens go.
They make up new words, say things quite absurd
(like they're always one step out of the herd),
forget all the rules that they learned in schools
or twist them or bend them like some darn fools.
The CAPitalize wrONG – or not at all,
push wordstogether or space   for   a   stall.

But, poets are artists who paint with words,
creating their visions with lines and curves.

The picture is set by the artist's hand
and should remain so, unless by command
of the one who put heart and mind on page –
Mess with their musings and poets will rage.

A (Sorta) Sonnet

Poetic Musings

Poetry as prism:

    emotional expectorant

    intellectual invigorator

    spiritual synthesizer

Poems:

    fingerprints of fantasy

    footsteps of ourstory

    hieroglyphic graffiti

Writing mothers:

    steal time during naps or when everyone's asleep

        to exercise their passion

    contract with themselves to fill daily quotas

        in quarter-hour increments

    exalt when something is actually completed

        and ready to stand on its own.

Untitled

Eventually it gets to the point where
I gotta stop tryin' to drown out the noise.

I mean, at first the radio works – and
for a while, it's only my own faucet
and drainpipes that I can hear.

But it grows somehow – or maybe my senses
just become irritated, and refuse to discount
the distant roar of airplanes and train engines and
the closer sounds of sirens and vehicles –

refuse to be soothed by denial any longer.

The radio must be silenced, and in its absence
the sounds of the city creep in to my space –
including barks and voices and…slamming doors.

I relinquish my ears to whatever besets them
and long for the silence of my own front yard
in the woods.

…But it is the sound of barely heard
arguments that most unnerves me – or

the scream of a child when I can't tell
whether it's game or pain that aroused it.

It's the slamming of doors, thrown gravel from
sharp turns and screeching brakes that break me…

Especially when I don't have the smooth,
easy sound of your breathing to keep me sane.

Coinsight

My schizo self becomes more in love

with

deep green peaceful country

and

bustling busy populated city

scenes

like going on a bus to dinner

with grandma, and then

staying with Cathy out at

Musselman's Lake.

I feel like a coin with two
entirely different sides.

I must learn to concentrate

    on the edge, on the circle

        uniting, joining the two.

Understandings

Stopping the Downward Spiral

Like many people, I have lived through times when life seemed unbearable in my current condition, and I didn't know how to move on or to stop my mind from taking me downward in a whirling confusion of fearful thoughts and emotions that grow darker by the moment.

Scary to feel like that, and even scarier when it seems unstoppable. You feel hopeless and powerless.

But those feelings became strong enough that I knew I had to do something.

Step one was learning to recognize that I was spiraling downward, developing greater awareness of my own thoughts and feelings.

Recognizing.

Re-cognizing. Cognition is mental awareness. Re-cognizing is becoming aware of something you already know.

Eventually you learn that if something doesn't change, the downward spiral will lead to collapse – physically, mentally, emotionally – after a possible explosion of tears and even howling.

You learn that you do not want to go down that way again.

But stopping it is not done by mere recognition, and reversing it on your own is nearly impossible.

I couldn't move myself from low to happy or hopeful. It was just too big a reach. Regardless of my desire for my own sake or the sake of others who were close to me, I could not just wish it away.

Eventually I learned that I could stop it, though, by making my thoughts repeat over and over:

Think good thoughts, Susan. Think good thoughts. Think good thoughts, Susan. Think good thoughts.

I couldn't think good thoughts right then, but I could stop the downward spiral. I could begin to breathe again and release the choking feeling of uncontrollable fear. Fighting off fear, overcoming it, has proven to be necessary for my mental and physical health.

When I was young and would be feeling sad or depressed, I used music to lift my mood. But I had to do it gradually, or it wouldn't work. I couldn't just play happy music and get happy. First, I would have to play sad songs that matched my dark mood. Then I would play something less melancholy, then a little lighter still, until I could play songs that were bright and happy. And my mood would be lifted.

Thoughts influence emotions, which influence behavior. Self-care is mental and emotional as well as physical. By learning to control our thoughts, and developing methodologies that work for us, we can figure out ways that we can help ourselves to **stop the downward spiral**.

Self-care is mental and emotional

as well as physical.

Dealing with Disappointment

You can be disappointed without being mad.

> Gratitude is a good antidote.
> Sometimes it's not easy to make that leap.
> But it is the better path.
> One way to try to relieve your disappointment is by blaming, whining and wailing.
> The other is to pause and realize that we each have a life, have our own values and ways.
> Learning to blend strengths and to build competence and confidence are life-long journeys.
> We might as well be kind to each other along the way.

Facing disappointment without bitterness has its benefits.

Whether it's not getting the promotion or recognition you felt you deserved or the gift you wanted, we all have opportunities to deal with disappointment.

Letting your feelings of disappointment linger and grow can lead to bitterness, anger and alienation.

You can recognize those feelings of disappointment and move on. Here's a few times I've had to do it.

Moving Across Country with My Love … and a Complete Stranger

Tom and I met when we lived halfway across the United States from each other, and we dated cross-country for over a year. The time had come for me to move out to Oklahoma, to his little cabin in the woods, to begin a life together. I'd been packing and sorting and selling and telling everyone I knew of my plans to move in with Tom, excited as can be.

When Tom pulled up at my home in Harrisburg, Pennsylvania, he wasn't alone. Riding with him was a scruffy-looking guy I'd never met. Confused, for sure, and pushing down questions getting in the way of my sheer delight, our greeting was more subdued than it might have been.

It turned out that the stranger was Tom's alcoholic friend who he pulled away from trouble and suicidal depression to come out to Oklahoma and help him in the shop, restoring old vehicles.

Dazed, all I could do was continue packing the last items and saying my last good-byes.

To say it changed how things were for us, driving across country in Tom's pickup truck and then living in Tom's little cabin with a room-mate, is the greatest understatement.

My heart, bursting with love and craving time alone with him, was disappointed time and again.

Had I let that turn into bitterness, we wouldn't be together now.

Sometimes a good cry helps.

We didn't have a phone when I first moved to Oklahoma, but I wanted to work as a substitute teacher, so we had a phone line put in. At first, it was a party line, connecting four area homes!

One afternoon when the phone rang, a woman's voice asked for Tom, and he greeted her as Candy. I knew this was his old girlfriend's name who lived in San Diego. He began the conversation by telling her my name and then proceeded to explain that I was living there with him.

My jaw dropped, my heart sank, and my feet headed for the door. I ran down towards the creek and then along the bank as fast and as far as I could. Then I fell into a heap and sobbed.

How could she not know? Why had he not told her???

I cried until I could not cry any more, then sat and watched the creek.

Tom found me eventually, put his arms around me, and after a long while we talked.

I say a good cry sometimes helps, not that it heals all wounds. In my profound disappointment and psychic exhaustion, I allowed the faith that I had that Tom was a good and honorable man to help me stand up and walk back to the cabin with him.

I can't say that I put this episode entirely aside, as the mention of her name brought a chill to my heart for years afterwards. I never forgot that he had not told her, but I eventually came to accept it. After decades together, the trust we have built far overshadows any doubt that was raised.

Turning aside from, turning away from bitterness is an important skill to develop, if you want to try to maintain a decent relationship with a loved one who has disappointed you.

The evolution of my prayers

I was taught to pray as a child, ritualized, memorized, in unison or silently reading along, and along the way, I'd done my share of pleading for help in dire straits or exclaiming God's name in surprising or disturbing circumstances. But my understanding of prayer and manner of prayer evolved slowly, through broader understanding of life.

That broader understanding was propelled in no small way by the experience and repercussions of having been violently assaulted and robbed. The physical damage of kicks to the head and shoulder area as I forced myself down into a corner of my vestibule, to keep from being pulled out the door, healed well. The elements of post-traumatic stress disorder can and do still surface decades later, though they were only recognized years after the assault, when I edited a dissertation on PTSD (Post Traumatic Stress Disorder).

Fear was something I definitely had to overcome. The first defense was moving into an apartment with my brother, Mark. The second was adopting a beautiful German shepherd, who let me enjoy nighttime walks along the river in Harrisburg with a freedom from fear I could not manage on my own. The dog continued to help me feel safe wherever we lived together.

Nikki died before I moved out into the woods in southeast Oklahoma. But I had been given a wonderful Golden Retriever who was gentle as could be, though he packed a strong, deep bark – a perfect combination for a canine friend. Dee Dog did not outlive my days in the deep woods, however, and overcoming fear when I was alone and Tom was off working or playing music was sometimes a real challenge.

The first prayer I developed and repeated often was:

> *Please, dear God, protect me from all harm.*

Before long, I expanded it to be:

Please, dear God, protect me from all harm,

especially that created by my own fear.

I had learned that what one focuses on or thinks about serves as an attractor. And I believed that if I focused on my fear, I would attract more circumstances that would re-enforce the fear.

I had also come to believe that life on a higher level – energy, spirit, spiritual beings, God, gods, angels, whatever you call the higher power or powers – can be called upon for help.

Like a faucet, if you don't believe and don't ask or crank it open, you won't get any of the good stuff. But ask, and you open the door for blessings, assistance, guidance, courage – what you need.

My prayer next developed to:

Please protect me from all harm, especially that created by my own fear, carelessness or ego.

That was added when I realized that losing focus while driving, or driving too fast to avoid being late for a meeting, could result in harm to me (or others), and that I could use some help with focusing and avoiding harm on such occasions. Repeating the prayer a few times helped me stay more focused, calm and aware of my driving.

One further evolution took into account that it wasn't only my own fear or carelessness that could cause me harm. I often start my prayers with "Please, dear God…" but sometimes I begin otherwise, or with no introduction. Begin as you wish, to call upon the forces of the universe you believe will offer help when you need it.

Please, dear God, protect me from all harm, especially that created by fear, carelessness or ego.

Another thing I learned along the way was to ask for the quality that I needed to face or to change a situation. It is me that my prayer can help, whether I am feeling the need to be stronger or smarter or wiser. Asking for help to be all that I can and need to be, not asking for a situation to be fixed for me.

In Oklahoma, I was driving to a meeting of statewide representatives, professional peers who included one woman who had viciously tried to turn my local associates against me, after we received a grant that she had applied for but not received. It was a devastating stab in the back from someone within an organization developed to care about and serve others. All the way during the three-and-a-half-hour drive to the meeting, I repeated to myself:

Please help me to be brave, and kind, and honest.

Whenever you are feeling lost and desperation is setting in, try to discover what would help you through. Asking for it helps you to focus on what you need to survive and overcome a situation, rather than focusing on the problem and how it might grow or develop bigger.

This is reinforced by a lesson from my husband, when he was teaching me to ride a motorcycle:

Don't look at the rock in the road! Look at where you want the wheel to go.

What a simple yet profound message.

Look at where you want YOUR wheel to go, and don't be afraid to reach out for assistance – from human and other beings who can help you live the life you want and deserve.

My newest prayer is simple and can be used in any situation you seek guidance for, or it can be said with the intention of sending helping thoughts towards/for another who is facing a difficult time:

Help me know what to do.

Help me do it well.

Inspired by Love

Mission Statement

I searched and thought while still a girl –
   What did I want most in the world?
What meant the most? What should I do?
   I thought and searched, until I knew.

And, for a while, as I learned life
   was full of trouble, pain and strife,
I floundered in my faith and hope.
   How could this be? How could I cope?

I struggled through a spirit quest –
   could God exist in all this mess?
And, if God did, how would I know?
   And why was war allowed to grow?

Then, in the quiet of the night,
   alone and in my room,
A thought came clear that seemed so right
   I've let it grow and bloom.

Out of my fear, my doubt and pain,
   a thought that's now my life's refrain,
From soul within or angel above:
   Yes, God exists, and God is love.

My job, then, was to live this faith –
   that love can overpower hate.
It was a message I should share –
   to show my God by how I care.

So, back then to my first true goal,
   set when I was a girl:
"To love and to be loved" was what
   I wanted in this world.

I learned love in my family,
   from parents fair and true;
But could I find love for myself?
   I hoped, but never knew....

Until I saw your face, my dear;
   Until I held you close and near.
Then all my doubt and pain and fear
   Vanished as our love came clear.

Our love's grown strong, our love is sure.
   Untarnished by all doubt, it's pure.
We won't hold back, we'll give and give
   as long as we should ever live.

All through this life, and life to come,
   Our love shines stronger than the sun.
Our job now is to love and share,
   To show our God by how we care.

You're The One
(Song)

You're the one I turn to.
You're the one I learn through.
You're the one who
Holds me when I cry.
You're the one who feeds me.
You're the one who needs me.
You're the reason it's easy to get by.

I don't know how it is
you do what you do.
All I do know is that
you love me, too.

≈ ≈ ≈ ≈

Together we will ride
the waves, the hills, the storms.
Together we face this life.
Together we sleep warm.

You're the one I turn to.
You're the one I learn through.
You're the one who
hears me when I roar.
You're the one who sees me.
You're the one who frees me.
You're the one I'll love forevermore.
Yes, you're the one I'll love forevermore.

Anniversary Sonnet

Because I have no independent wealth
  to buy you gifts so rare or fun or fine,
I offer you my words, my work and health,
  and joy as your eternal valentine.

If I were rich, I'd buy you splendid things,
  I'd lavish you with all you want or need,
And bring you sails or wheels or golden wings.
  Instead, you get this humble lover's creed.

My love is yours forever, darling man.
I am your truest, most devoted fan.
I'll share with you my days and nights and years,
laugh gladly with you, let you kiss my tears.
As on the day we wed, I do and will,
and when we leave this earth, I'll love you still.

Saying No

Saying "No"

Sometimes in life an offer comes along that seems at first glance to be the solution you've been looking for or an opportunity that is too good to pass up.

Sometimes we may need to quell the qualms of internal discomfort to even consider the possibility, but we try to ignore them and look at the bright side. It may a desire for fortune or fame, reaching for the golden ring, or fear of missing the train that would take you to your dream destination in life.

Sometimes when you ignore the qualms, though, you are only depriving yourself of the chance to avoid a disaster or to miss out on some misery.

Or, you may be going so hard down the road on a course you've set for yourself that you ignore warning signs and disregard or not have the energy for an alternative that would have been much better.

Sometimes it's hard to say no, especially when enticed or encouraged by someone or some people you feel ties with and may even love (or think you do).

There are times in my life when NO would likely have been the better choice, but thankfully there are others when it was the right choice, and I made it.

A sense of internal discomfort sometimes helps me decide. Sometimes it is a warning sign.

I started to pay more attention to what is referred to as gut-level reactions after a visit to a store in Kansas City that was called Bob's Bizarre Bazaar. They had some earring findings, and I wanted nice hooks to make a pair for a present. The Bazaar was attached to a collection of shops, and Tom and our friend Jamey went into the center court to order some lunch for us.

The shop had things that were odd, like shrunken heads and other things seemingly related to black magic and witchcraft. I cruised the store looking for jewelry supplies, and as I walked around, a sense of nausea grew stronger the longer I was in there. I felt like I was suffocating and getting ready to vomit. I left hurriedly, glad to have the door close behind me and to see Tom and Jamey sitting and laughing together. I told them how "creeped out" I had been in the shop, vowing never to return.

Several months later, the KC newspapers started reporting about the owner of that shop having body parts buried in his yard and in his freezer, evidence that was found in a police search after a young man who was his next intended victim escaped from him.

After that, I started paying more attention to physical reactions to situations. And it has become helpful in making difficult decisions.

My nephew was in a bit of a quandary as he approached graduating from Drexel University with an engineering degree. Alex had done volunteer work bringing water to a village in Central America and he was hoping to work on designing eco-friendly buildings. But it was 2008, and the economic collapse had closed the door to working in construction. A railroad company offered him a job, but he was drawn towards joining the Peace Corps instead. His dad suggested that he call me.

We talked a while, and it was obvious he was really torn, as he sincerely wanted to do both.

One thought I shared with him was that if he worked for a while before he joined the Peace Corps, not only would he have an opportunity to learn more that might be helpful to his work in the Peace Corps, he would also have solid work experience on his resume when he was ready to return to the work force.

I also shared a method I'd developed for myself (that has since become a bit of a family joke). I told him when I had a really difficult decision to make, I'd "decide" to do A, and let that sit for a while. Giving that choice my attention would result in either feeling comfortable and ready to start planning and preparing, or acid would start rising in my throat.

Later, when his dad asked Alex if he'd talked to me, he said he had, and when Mark inquired further, he said, "Aunt Skeebee makes her decisions based on her indigestion."

I laughed out loud when Mark told me that, but it was pretty accurate. It's one thing I had discovered in learning to trust my gut, that acid rising in my throat could not only cause but also be caused by discomfort.

(And now you know my family nickname. Thanks to my older brother, Rick!)

A more recent time that this proved helpful was when I was offered work when I really could have used some, from one of my first clients, a man I really enjoyed working with and respected. He was an accountant, and I'd edited his dissertation many years ago. This new editing work would be for a novel that he had written. I asked to see a sample of the work, to see the extent of editing required before I accepted or gave him a proposal for doing the job.

The novel was dark from the beginning, the story of scientists creating and then trying to control an increasingly violent and monstrous animal. The further I read, the more my shoulders stooped forward and my head started to hang.

I wanted to help my former client, and I could have used the work. But I just could not do it.

I didn't want to leave him in the lurch, and fortunately, I had a friend and fellow editor who also needed work. I introduced them, and they have developed into a productive team, resulting in several published novels.

Shortly afterward, I was contacted by Orla Hazra, a former would-be client who had been working on her doctoral dissertation at Fordham University when we first met. We spoke then about her editing needs, and I recommended that she find someone who was already familiar with Fordham's dissertation guidelines.

Orla had a new editing project, and it was just the kind of material I wanted to immerse myself in. She is one of the founders of the

Deeptime Network, and her personal and professional history is amazing.

Had I accepted the novel, I may not have been able to take on her project. My NO was the right choice.

In a podcast interview on Apple, Tom Hanks was talking about his new book and his career, and he slipped in a bit of advice to those coming up behind him in the acting profession. It wasn't said as though it should be printed on a poster or a bumper sticker, but it struck me as something that deserves to be shared and remembered, and I am happy to pass it along to you:

"Say NO to those things you don't want to do."

Tom Hanks

Inspired by Love Too

Ode to an Adoptive Grandmother

A mother knows her daughter's heart.
    She's watched it grow right from the start.
        She's seen her laugh and run and play,
            rest in the night, stretch through the day.

And when this child's to woman grown
    and wants a daughter of her own,
        her mother hopes she, too, can know
            the joy of watching baby grow.

Sometimes it seems this joy won't come.
    Hopes dashed so often start to numb.
        The eggs won't grow, or die stillborn.
            And dreams do fade in hearts forlorn.

Then comes a chance to adopt a child,
    and hope's reborn, and dreams are wild.
        But mother fears for daughter's heart –
            if this should fail, will it tear apart?
As days grow short, this fear grows strong.
    She longs to hear her daughter's song
        of love and joy, of glee and mirth,
            of legal mother, of healthy birth.

And when it is all settled down,
      she changes grandchild's sleeping gown.
           She glows with pride, her hope's complete.
               She watches daughter kiss tiny feet.

                                  Mother's Day, 1997

Primary Love

I love your little primary color splashes
   left along our pathways.
Brown, earthen pathways and deep green leaves
   are well accentuated by your blocks and balls.

Your shopping cart is overturned, lying the same way
   you toppled it when you first played with it,
Straddling the basket and spinning the wheels,
   grumbling out racecar sounds and looking gleeful.

I like to come across them as I walk the paths alone,
   you napping nearby, safely on your pillow.
They are so welcome. You are so welcome. We are so
   thankful you are here with us, to bring us
      joy and work and love and color.

Almost 2

Looking through your outgrown garments,
    I snuggle one to my face,
        embracing your yesterday's
        smallness and everyday's warmth.

You squealed with delight at this darling little blouse,
    before you'd even worn it,
        when you could hardly sit upright,
            watching me fill the clothesline
        with our newly washed clothes.
Knowing no words, but oh, so effective with your sounds,
    hugging it to you, "Oooooohhh"-ing appreciatively,
        you shine with love of beauty.

You often help choose your best outfits, and
    enthusiastically go through bags of clothes with me
    or solo if I'm busy doing other things.

You look good in good clothes.
    You look cozy in comfy clothes.
        You look great in hats.
    Sunglasses suit you wonderfully well.

        Your fascination – with necklaces, earrings,
        motorcycles and tractors – is mesmerizing.

Almost 2, Too

You love going faster & higher in the swing, spinning,
    hanging upside down – you thrill seeker,
      you enjoyer of attention while you enjoy these things.

Your first "trick" was to throw yourself backwards,
    holding on to my hands and landing on my legs
        and then pulling yourself upward.
    You grinned at your dad ("See me?"), such a teeny, tiny girl.

But fortunately, you also have a strong sense of caution,
    And wisdom.
    Like telling us when you found a broken glass, for instance,
Or like you used to call when you saw matches anywhere,
      "Away, [put] away!"

I'm sure you will test all our limits. I'm trying to ready myself.
    Your dad & I will try to decide how far you can safely go,
        Until you are flying on your own
        (which seems like it won't be long).

    We'll work to give you all the room you need
        to try your wings
        within the expanding circle of our love.

Listen to Your Body or It Might Get Loud

My Body Lessons

> You need sleep
>
> Good nutrition builds good health AND comfort
>
> Wear shoes that fit
>
> Practice good injury management
>
> Balance work / rest for muscles + joints

You need sleep.

My body lessons have been a source of insight and inspiration, and among the important lessons was that sleep and health are closely related.

Like many students, I was sleep deprived in my college days, and I was sick with increasing frequency. No stranger to swollen glands and rounds of antibiotics, I'd gone through them all of my days. But the cycle was starting to interfere more with things I wanted and needed to do, with days of in-bed and on-medication recuperations. I would get thoroughly wiped out, and strep throat was a regular diagnosis. I reached the point as graduation neared when I said, "Something has to change."

Researching swollen glands, infections and how to avoid them became an avocation, and it was the start of my gathering information on herbs and natural medicine.

One thing I noticed was that the problem usually began slowly, reaching its full, debilitating potential if I did not listen to my body and ignored the feeling that I was starting to get a sore throat. The swelling of glands in my throat became a sign that it was time to slow down or trouble was ahead. Sleep became a higher priority, and if I heard and heeded the signals, I could often get by with a couple of good sleeps instead of days and nights of being ill.

You might think that sleeping more would be no problem, but I have been sleep resistant all my life. I remember reading by the light coming in from a narrow crack in my bedroom door, allowed so I would not have to sleep in the pitch dark. I hurried into bed when I heard my parents come upstairs, then often returned to the floor to read long after they were quiet for the night.

I went through extended spells when 6 hours was a good strong sleep for me, and I often got less. Sleep is still something I almost always put off until it seems entirely necessary, though once in a while I allow exhaustion to bring me to bed for an early night or to excuse a rare morning sleep-in.

I did come to respect it much more when I was trying to lose weight a few years ago and read that getting enough sleep was important in that effort. I set a goal of getting 7 hours of sleep each night, and along with other lifestyle changes, I was able to lose weight.

Recently I saw an interview with Johann Hari, author of "Stolen Focus," in which he explained that sleep was the time that the waste products from your awake-brain activities were flushed out of the brain and moved on into the body's elimination system. That may help explain some of the brain fog that sets in when we let ourselves get too sleep deprived.

Sleep gives the body the opportunity to fully relax. Muscles can release, and that can help the spine realign. I went through an afternoon and evening recently when pain flashed across the whole right rear section of my skull intermittently, strong enough to make me wince and lose my concentration. Though it was strong enough to be concerning, I realized it was a nerve issue and hoped that it could be resolved when the spine moved and released the pinched nerve. That night while I slept, it did. The next day I experienced a few shadow sensations, but no more pain. Sweet sleep benefits us in so many ways.

……………..

While I was a student at Duquesne University, I became involved in the grape boycott initiated by the United Farm Workers. I learned that all food was not equal, that some carried agricultural toxins that were harmful.

Workers were being sprayed in the field and poisonous chemicals remained on and in grapes carried by Pittsburgh grocers, where I handed out flyers and pleaded with Saturday morning shoppers to support the boycott by not buying grapes.

Thus began my interest in natural, organically grown food, which has continued and grown over the years. This interest was nurtured as I began to study and gather information from sources devoted to natural and/or alternative health. Information on preventing and treating infections, and information on psoriasis – a condition I'd had for many years. Both areas converged in promoting natural food and healthy diet.

My diet changed over time as I progressed through an education on my personal health issues and natural health treatments. Through reading and personal experience, I learned what foods or combinations of foods might aggravate or soothe my body, and I tried to eat as well as I could.

Better food choices over the years have proven to me as well as others:

Good Nutrition builds good health AND comfort.

As my diet improved, I experienced relief from another issue that had caused me great discomfort over the years. As a child, painful episodes of constipation sometimes resulted in suppository insertions, with intermittent times of extremely loose bowels. Looking back, some of that problem may well have been related to the frequent antibiotic regimens I was prescribed for repeated bouts of swollen tonsils and glands in my neck – my gut biome had to be a mess.

Don't expect to discover or achieve a magic formula for eating just right for your body. Bodies change over time, and so do food preferences, needs and tolerances.

I went through a period in my childhood when eating eggs resulted in my burping out an obnoxious gas that smelled and tasted rotten, like sulfur. Believe me, I avoided eggs for a long time. Eventually, I was able to re-introduce them into my diet by starting with a bit of hard scrambled egg. (Recent reading led me to information about a sulfur-type reaction to some antibiotics at the time I had the problem.)

Another example of changing tolerance was my inability to eat fruits and vegetables at the same meal without getting indigestion. It was with me for a long while, much to my chagrin when someone prepared a salad that included beautiful fresh strawberries or blueberries. I kept trying occasionally, and now I have become less sensitive to adding some fruit to a meal that has a lot of vegetables. But it still often seems better, out of an abundance of caution, for me to avoid veg-fruit combinations.

While physical comfort afforded by reasonable weight and the smooth digestion and elimination of food are some of the benefits of good diet, the pleasure afforded by good, clean food goes well beyond health and comfort to provide real pleasure.

Sometimes when I see a shopper hovering over carrot choices, I take the opportunity to say that if they ever want to know about the benefits of paying a bit more for organic produce, they should buy and eat a pound of organic carrots, and then another, and then buy a pound of regular carrots. The difference in taste will be glaringly obvious.

Clean food is healthier, tastes better and is so much better for the environment. When I buy organic produce, I am supporting the organic farming industry. When I buy grass-fed, whole milk dairy products, I am supporting dairy operations that follow more sustainable practices resulting in healthier livestock. The same applies to grass-fed beef. Those animals absorb vitamin D from the sun, and they pass it along in their milk and meat products.

The bonus is that extra money it costs for us to eat clean and natural food is money we do not give to doctors.

I'm not a purist when it comes to dining out or eating what someone else has cooked, and not every ingredient in my home is organic. But when I am making the choice, organic is what I select – except sometimes when the selection is poor and the organic product is terribly overpriced.

....

Psoriasis became an issue for me during my high school years. My scalp would have patches of itchy, raised skin that would come off in flakes when scratched. I thought it was and treated it as dandruff at first, but then my elbows and knees broke out with active psoriatic patches.

Medical doctors informed us that they could not tell us what caused the condition or how to rid my body of it. They did say they knew of one oral medication that had some success in controlling outbreaks, but it would require me to limit exposure to sunlight to mere minutes a day. As a teenager with fairly close access to Atlantic Ocean beaches, that did not appeal to me at all.

With ointments and creams, and nasty smelling tar-based shampoos, I was able to keep the problem to a minimum. Until, that is, right before high school graduation, when I broke out from the neck down in red welts that resembled the measles but settled into a body-wide outbreak of psoriasis. Itchy, ugly. Proms were ahead, and graduation.

Every Spring my school put on a big show, with chorus and dance and orchestra performances. We were changing into costumes in our home rooms (all-girls school) for a rehearsal when a girl standing behind me let out a big scream. I turned to see what had frightened her and realized she was looking at me. The big red welts had turned to silvery, flaky patches that were peeling off my back. I laughed as I grabbed my blouse and headed towards the door, then cried in the bathroom.

My mom made my gowns, because there were none available to buy with high necklines and long sleeves. She made a beautiful soft blue gown with blue lace sleeves and bodice, and another one that had a white dotted sheer overdress, with a bright pink underdress for my boyfriend's prom and a white underdress for graduation, enabling me to attend these events without embarrassment. That awful neck-to-toe outbreak happened to me a second time, right before I graduated from college.

As part of my research on preventing and treating repeated infections, I came across the medical psychic Edgar Cayce's work. In one trance reading for a person suffering from psoriasis, Cayce went into dietary recommendations, and I came away with the new understanding that gut health was a factor in my skin problem. What a concept!

Recent studies are finally now showing a relationship between diet and psoriasis, with recommendations coming forth from institutions as venerable as Johns Hopkins Medicine about eliminating inflammatory foods from your diet to help control the symptoms of psoriasis.

My understanding is that the walls of the intestines are too thin, allowing toxins to pass through into the blood stream.

My body functions best on a clean, healthy diet – with room for indulgences.

……………….

My body also wants shoes that fit comfortably, and it lets me know that wearing anything else results in physical discomfort – from annoying to nearly crippling.

My feet were fairly spoiled by good parents who could afford good shoes and who felt that investing in something durable was worthwhile. The four babies born to my mother all benefitted from good footwear, at least until our adolescence when fashion often over-ruled sensibility and durability.

Shoes were prescribed as a therapy for me, too, to try to overcome my walking with the front of my left foot thrown out to the side, which manifested after I learned to walk a second time before the age of 3.

My brother and I had been fussing in the car before we stopped at a grocery store. He was trying to give me a make-up hug when he climbed up on the side of the grocery cart where I was seated. At that time, child seats were outside the grocery basket, between the handles. We crashed to the floor, and my left leg broke just below the hip. After a long period in traction, I had to build up muscle and learn how to crawl and then walk again.

When I've worn ill-fitting shoes, my feet complain and other parts of my body may suffer as well – due to things like spinal alignment and/or muscle guarding issues. Toes can get misshapen and toenails can develop issues that can cause pain and concern.

Clothes that fit comfortably are another thing my body really appreciates, and it will talk to me when I don't wear them. Tightness in the wrong spots leads to irritation, which I definitely try to avoid. Along with many others, appreciation for my "softies" has grown in the last few years with more time at home. When necessary, any of us will suffer a bit with less than comfortable shoes or clothes for the sake of our image, professional or otherwise, but overall, my body lesson is:

Wear shoes and clothes that fit.

....

Practice good injury management.

That's a body lesson that I've had plenty of opportunity to learn and re-learn.

Little remembered childhood bumps, cuts and bruises were topped off with two well remembered bicycle-involved incidents in which my left knee was dragged along the ground in areas covered with cinders. They soured my interest in bicycles.

Over the years I've learned that having a good collection of bandages, wraps, ointments and creams goes a long way towards being able to manage the skin injuries. Scrapes, cuts and burns deserve to be taken seriously or they can turn into ugly problems.

My preference is for natural salves and Sovereign Silver®, with some use of antimicrobial ointment when appropriate or prescribed. I have a salve a friend makes with arnica and CBD, and it is great on sore muscles. I have another with jewelweed that is great for insect bites and poison ivy blisters. And I still have a bit of wound-care salve made by Dr. Tiarona Low Dog when I went to her ranch in New Mexico a few years ago for a training in natural first aid.

One example of listening to my body was following an incident in which hot oil that I spilled burned my right hand so badly that an emergency room trip was required. As soon as it happened, I plunged my hand into ice water and kept it in there all the way to the hospital. My instinct to keep it in that ice water was reinforced when I had to remove my hand to let ER folks take a look at it – I could have screamed in pain.

The ER staff treated it and bandaged it extensively, creating a mitten-like surrounding of soft gauze. Whenever I took it out of the protection to clean and treat the blisters across my three outside fingers and the big knuckles along the back of my hand, it was clear that getting back into that cloud of protection ASAP was strongly desired. Even when the plastic surgeon treating me said, more than once, that it didn't really need that much bandaging, I kept applying it, until the hand felt ready for smaller bandages towards the end of the healing period.

Though injuries are best treated as soon as possible, some do go undetected and/or untreated for a long time. Once in a while, they can still be healed.

One injury/issue that left me no choice but to seek help was revealed through a terrible bout of sciatica pain. I couldn't tell whether it was soft tissue problem created, as it didn't seem to be centered in my hip area, so I started with some active release treatments to see if soft-tissue work would help. It brought some relief temporarily, but I began to get the sense that it was more related to a structural problem.

I'd heard lots of good things about one local chiropractor, so I started seeing him. He immediately determined that one leg was shorter than the other, and that the whole spine was fairly out of alignment. He aligned my hips, informing me that their misalignment caused the difference in my leg length, and he adjusted my spine on up my back, ending with the neck. My whole body felt changed, freer. The next time I saw him, he said that my walk was totally different, that my hips were no longer locked. We kept working together, and things were slowly improving. I loved reading the charts he had on the walls. One weekend (it always happens on a weekend, doesn't it?), my sciatica pain level rose incredibly, and it felt like my big toe wanted to blow off.

When I explained that to Dr. Arme, he said, "That sounds like the nerve that comes out between the lowest vertebrae and the sacrum."

I was standing in front of the treatment table. He gently felt the base of my spine, and then said, "Your last vertebrae is twisted and off its base. Let me see what I can do."

I could feel a gentle pressure, like a massage, as he worked on it. "There, that's the twist," he said, and then, "there, it's back on its base."

My knees buckled and the difference I felt as I walked out of his office a few minutes later was nearly dizzying.

My soft tissue, of course, was not happy with being displaced from where it had grown used to being, and it pulled the spine back to where it was as best it could. So, Dr. Arme and I had regular appointments for a while, as my body learned a new structural alignment.

Then there were the injury appointments, like after the automatic garage door came down on my head and knocked me on my ass – crunching my spine from both ends. Dr. Arme was my first call. And the time I faceplanted rounding a corner of the fence too quickly to keep my balance, landing teeth first on a large plastic planter – thankfully full and secure on the ground, breaking my fall without breaking my teeth, head or neck!

Long trips in the automobile would prompt me to see Dr. Arme beforehand, and afterward, as my body does not like to sit for long periods and the jostle of the road can leave my spine out of balance.

I would go to him when I started "walking crooked," because I knew I was out of whack, and the problem would travel up the spine. It often starts with a bit of numbness under my left foot if I walk too long. If I go for a treatment soon enough, we can catch it when it has only messed things up to my mid-back. If not, it will progress to my neck and get that out of line, too, creating further problems.

Other Spine Related Body Lessons

My first understanding of the importance of the spine to other, seemingly unrelated aspects of health happened long ago.

Back pain has been an issue for me, though for a long time it was largely unrecognized. All my life, I've stretched and bent and moved my body more than most people, as it really seemed to need it. When Tom and I got together, he would "roll me" by wrapping his arms around my back at my waist as we faced each other and then gently lift and pull up. Often my back would crack, and I would feel instant relief. Sometimes we used other methods, like standing back-to-back with arms locked, then him leaning forward and lifting me, arching his back and rounding my back.

My first strong lesson had to do with indigestion. I would suddenly experience serious indigestion with no obvious cause. I may not have eaten for hours, had no recent bowel issues, but serious, unexplained nausea and indigestion would come up. Somehow, one of our spine adjustment sessions aligned with one of these nausea periods, and when my back cracked, the nausea ceased. Utterly amazed and incredibly pleased, I decided to try it again when another attack came along, and sure enough, it again corrected the problem. I realized that there is a spot in my spine that sets off a nausea sensation when it is out of alignment.

The next lesson involved energy, focus, full awareness and clarity.

One day when I was standing talking with Tom, I felt my neck crack - and my eyes flew open. I immediately felt like I was functioning at full capacity, and I realized that my eyes had been drooped half-shut and my energy and focus had been dimmed. The next time it happened, I was convinced that it was a place in my neck that puts me at half-mast when it is out of line. I've developed the ability to recognize the symptoms and do some neck stretches and self-massage to help open things up for an easy re-alignment, and I don't expect too much of myself until the neck cracks in just the right spot and things are back in place.

Sometimes I wish I were better at it, able to self-adjust whenever I need to, but sometimes the body takes a while to release and self-correct. And as my friend MaryJane once told me, "You can take care of the easy stuff yourself, Susan, but for the big stuff, outside assistance is needed."

A Word About Chiropractors

Let me begin by saying unequivocally: Dr. Arme changed my life. He fixed a problem that had kept my body misaligned for 70 years, and he has helped me and many friends upon multiple occasions.

He was not my first experience with chiropractors. One convinced me that I needed to sign up for, and pre-pay for, a series of treatments that would be more than once a week for several months. He had his patients use some equipment before each session, and each session was brief and repetitive. He is the kind that gives the profession a bad name, along with those who truly do not connect with their patients and the few who may indeed do harm.

Dr. Arme begins every appointment by having you describe how you are feeling right then, and you tell him of any problems you've had since your last visit. He works with how your body is at the moment. He is gentle and instructive, the very essence of what I admire and seek in a health care provider.

My sister-in-law was having back pain, and I called Dr. Arme's office for a referral. The office staff gave me the name of a chiropractor in her vicinity who went to the same school and had the same equipment as Dr. Arme. She found much relief through treatments received through that referral.

One more spine lesson is related to a condition that had a remarkable reaction to a simple crack in the right spot in my neck. At times over the last several years, I've had a day of full-on sinus production, blowing my nose constantly as my sinuses sent flows out of my body. They weren't days of illness, I learned after a bit. And usually, they only lasted one day. I would say that I'd had a one-day cold, because the next day, I'd be fine.

Studying the charts on the walls waiting for Dr. Arme to come into the treatment room, I saw that C2 had an influence on sinuses, and I know we'd worked on C2 issues. He confirmed that if that joint were out of alignment, it could very well impact my sinuses.

After that, when those days come on, I work on massaging and stretching my neck, to try to crack it in the right spot. If I can do that, my sinuses immediately cease production. It takes a bit to clear things out, but the flood stops. It is truly amazing.

Listening to my body and learning about my body, I've been able to manage a condition that is rather disruptive to my comfort and productivity. Unfortunately, it's not like I have the magic trigger figured out. It often takes a lot of stretching and movement before the right little crack happens.

Looking over Dr. Arme's charts again recently, I could relate to something in most spine related issues listed for each vertebrae connection. As I thought about that, it occurred to me that since the very lowest vertebrae in my spine had been out of place for most of my life, it would make sense that none of my vertebrae were quite properly aligned, until the base problem was resolved. No wonder so many spine-effected issues seemed familiar to my own medical history.

Once in a while, your body may scream at you like mine did many years ago, driving me to the emergency room in time to have my appendix removed before it burst inside me.

Do what you can when you can to keep yourself comfortable and healthy, but seek help when your body starts to get loud. Medical professionals have much to offer in times of illness and disease, but remember:

Monitoring and improving your health is your job. If you take that job seriously, it is more likely that you will stay healthy and find the right help when you need it.

Good Changes
(Song)

May all our changes be good changes.
May every step lead us on
further down the road as we travel,
learning as we go, leaving love when we're gone.

From our first breath to our last,
life never stays the same.
Change is what we get.
It's the only game.
You think you've got *your spot* in this lifetime,
Or maybe you feel stranded in a rut…But,
All that you take in serves to change you,
in your brain, in your heart and in your gut.

May all your changes be good changes.
May every step lead you on
further down the road as you travel,
learning as you go, leaving love when you're gone.

Every choice that you make,
every food that you eat
brings more to your life than you may know.
Every picture you see,
every sound that comes in
shapes the way you think and grow.

May all our changes be good changes.
May every step lead us on
further down the road as we travel,
learning as we go, leaving love when we're gone.
Learning as we go, leaving love when we're gone.

Pondering Life and Death

Parallel Excavations

A gas explosion in a Colorado coal mine
  traps men beneath the earth
    as the shaft collapses
on the east coast, my father's body
        is wracked with abdominal pain
      (deep, shifting, pain)

The miners approach the disaster slowly
  uncertain of continued collapse
    caught between instincts
my father's aching body is examined cautiously
       (X-rayed, manipulated, interrogated)
        for the unknown breakdown

They pick away at the surface debris
  then start to move the rubble away carefully
    balancing speed and caution
the source of physical suffering is elusive
       (no picture or poke can determine)
       evading external evaluation

Delicately they dig deeper, damning time
  the process of rescue seems endless
    so slow, so uncertain of success
surgery is prescribed to determine the cause
            several options are proposed
        others are left unsaid

The wait seems endless for the families
  standing by helplessly, hopingly, coping
    with fear for a loved one's life

As they dig into the bowels of the earth
  surgeons explore the cavern of my father's belly,
    probing for the life-threatening leak
      which is found in the lower intestine.

As my father lay pale, moaning, recovering,
Fifteen dead miners will be buried again.

Death, be not proud

Sometimes, dear Death, your kiss is sweet,
      from pain and suffering you bring relief.
But even then, you leave the loss
      and each who loved must bear the cost.

Sometimes, oh Death, you enter slow,
      your presence known before the woe.
But even then, the time's unsure
      and one succumbs to hope of cure.

Sometimes, dark Death, you snatch from womb.
      Unknown, the soul goes to the tomb.
But though some people feel the pain,
      they know not who lies 'neath the rain.

But when, cursed death, you strike as now,
      when, without warning, your grasp most foul,
You engulf a youth so loved and kind,
      you leave your stain on heart and mind.
You seem most cruel, most mad, and blind.

When one could fly through air, as he,
      and was so fine and fair as he,

Why could you not withhold your touch until

      he'd lived and loved and laughed his fill?

Cursèd Death, may the taste of this victory be bitter.

Half-Year Reflections

You're on my mind and in my heart today.
The sadness turns each breath into a sigh,
then a labor…sucking in…releasing…
My throat tightens, tears well up and spill.

Soon, a warmth begins to grow in my heart.
Spreading, it calms my breathing and my soul.
Thoughts and feelings clear and focus on you,
on the tremendous love I feel for you.

I hope you can know now how completely
and deeply I love you and cherish you,
All doubts and misgivings left far behind.

Can you see into my heart and my mind,
and feel how this love sweetly warms my life?

Gone half a year, I miss you every day.
For your eternal peace and joy I pray.

Since Mom Died...

No one to be brave for anymore,

No one to prove to that you can still do it.

No one to complain about the floor,

Or to tell you to take it easy.

Lightning crashes, rain rains down in sheets,

You lay in your bed in the middle of the day.

It came on so quickly it seems

You were fine, you were strong, you were active,

Then illness, sadness, loneliness, and finally pain.

It's the pain that's done you in, draining you of desire

To continue on with your life.

You had wanted to live to be 100, and I had cheered.

I don't think you hold that goal anymore, and I don't blame you.

You rest. I weep.

Sweet soul released

Sweet soul released
      from the bonds of space and time,
Look back briefly
      to see how much you are loved.
Then fly on, into eternity,
      your spirit now free
           To live and grow forever.

Reflections

Heart to Heart

We all operate differently.

Our unique experiences result in an un-replicated life.

Our experience shapes us, which influences the way we experience life. Events lost in deep memory still shade our understanding of the universe and our reactions to future events.

Influence. Shape. They do not dictate.

We select activities and can choose those that keep us going down the same path or those that will help us move in a different direction.

It's up to us to decide.

Each day brings opportunities to choose health and love. We need to be open minded and open hearted enough to recognize them and let them in.

Feelings of sadness, sorrow, frustration and a sense of limitation, thoughts that seem to drag us down – these things will happen. They are a part of life. But they need not define our life. We are bigger than that – we can be bigger.

Not only do we each have experiences that no one else has had, we each have our own way of being, our own awareness, unique memories and ways of remembering.

You know of the experiments where multiple people see an accident and each report it differently. They each remember it differently. Same facts, different information details taken in and remembered.

My way of taking things in and processing them became more obvious to me when I attended monthly game nights with a group of women. I only knew the woman who invited me to join the gatherings. I knew little of the other women's history, so many of their stories didn't stick, as I didn't know the players.

When I thought back on an evening with them, my memory perspective became clear after time spent trying to recall what some of them were wearing. I realized that I couldn't recall many details at all. Sometimes I could get the color, and then other details might return. But I could easily relate to you how each of them was feeling that night. Whether they were frustrated with a spouse or child, drained from dealing with their own or a loved one's health issue, or feeling good and upbeat. I could remember feelings.

I have a strong emotional memory. The rest of remembering takes some work on my part.

So, please forgive me if I don't recall some detail of a conversation we had that was very important to you. And tell me about it, remind me about it and let me know what it has meant to you.

But, if I don't remember what I said to you, it is likely that we were speaking heart-to-heart. When we are, my mind and memory are secondary. If I said something you needed to hear, it was my spirit responding to your spirit, and sometimes messages come through that weren't meant for me to remember and cherish.

The universe will offer us what we need, if we acknowledge the need, the desire, and ask for the strength, grace, intelligence or whatever we need to receive it and benefit from it.

Some of my early prayers began with "Please, dear God, if it is your holy will…" My way of asking for help but acknowledging that I might not know what is truly best for me. This was started when I was asking about something that would be truly life-changing.

I find it most helpful to ask for qualities (strength, wisdom, patience, etc.) I need to face or improve a situation, rather than divine intervention to fix. And I know that when we ask for help, we have to take the steps that will lead us in the direction we want to go.

Spiritual energy surrounds us, but like the water in the spigot,

it is accessed only by opening the faucet,

by asking for assistance, support

or guidance.

Appreciate Abundance

"Everything we experience starts in the mind.

Think about Orville and [Wilbur] Wright. They first imagined an airplane in their mind, then they drew what was in their mind and then built it."

Jane Barr

There was a time in our lives when debt had mounted to a scary level, and fear had started to emerge. Discomfort when paying bills, juggling income and watching expenses rise became the norm. Trying to figure out how to get past it and get out of the hole was beyond me at the time.

It was something said by my good friend Jane Barr during one of the long walks and talks we used to enjoy regularly when we lived close together that turned my attitude, my thinking and my future in a better direction.

She spoke to me of abundance, and the need to see abundance, to think in terms of abundance, and to truly appreciate it. Gratitude was the key to more blessings.

I took it in intellectually, though it didn't really resonate with me just then.

But the next time I paid bills, I found my way from internal grumbling to thinking about and feeling gratitude for the fact that at least we had enough income to pay that month's bills! It relieved me of some of the burdensome feelings of worry and doubt.

And the time after that, I did the same.

Slowly, gratitude grew and my thinking changed.

So did our financial situation. I took a hard look at our financial situation and grew more diligent in planning for and saving for expenses. We juggled debt a bit to take advantage of rate specials.

And work came in that kept me busy and kept credit card debt diminishing, until it was gone!

We are all co-creators, and it all starts in the mind and heart.

Appreciate abundance.

Gratitude Prayers

Try to say "Thank you" prayers every chance you get.

It will open your heart and life to more blessings.

A beautiful sunset.

A warm hug or smile shared with a friend.

A good meal.

Thank you.

Remember: The universe is full of blessings.

Even the hard times can bring good lessons.

When you give a gift, and it is well received, it brings you joy and makes you more inclined to offer further gifts.

Gratitude grows.

Be sure to say "Thank you" prayers much more often than "Please..."prayers.

Life has many opportunities and delivers many blessings.

Focus on the joy, and the joy will multiply.

Inspired

In Praise of Sunset Visions

The clouds were like a symphony of color,
   gorgeous, glorious, golden hues,
  heavenly shades of roses and blues,
   floating fantastic formations.

They moved slowly, seeming to advance
   majestically, mystically, magically,
  heavenly visions of prayers pursued
   through the dazzling, dew-gathered dance.

Lightning lit dramatic virtuosos,
   Responding energies reuniting.

The visions seemed to show themselves,
   then melt and fade into visions anew,
  speaking silent secret sights
   of what I am to do.

To Oliver

To Oliver
For the Inexpressible
With Gratitude

like the strong, African sun
radiant, rich, life-giving force
feeding the fertile ground
with the energy of your/self

forming from fecund matter
food for the eyes, ears, mind, heart
the clay of the earth combining
creating life-luscious art

strong and sure as deep ocean tides,
sonorous as the wandering wind,
you call to life the dormant seeds
that each of us holds within

strong, African son,
sing your song universal.
Pour forth your golden warmth.
As we bathe in the light of your eyes,
our skies have new horizons.

Sea Love

For Brother John
(Song)

There's a man
who sails the sea.
Living on the water
he feels free, he feels free.

With the wind
and with the sun,
the fish and birds, he don't
need anyone, not anyone.

Ride the waves
and feel the wind
take you to that place where
no man's ever been, no man's been.

Watch the gulls
go gliding by,
riding currents you can't see
in the sky, in the sky.

Watch the clouds
go rolling past,
sometimes slowly and sometimes
dark and fast, dark and fast.

See the stars
up in the sky.
Ain't the moon so pretty
it makes you want to cry.

Sail on, sail on,
Sail into the lonely waters
Towards the sun.

Sail on, my brother, sail on,
alone in this world
until your journey's done.
Your journey's been well done.

Sailor's Wife's Song

When Johnny-Boy goes off to sea,
Oh, what then shall I do?
He'll learn to love the sea, and me,
I'll learn to love it, too.

For the only thing a sailor's wife
can do to appease the worry and strife,
is to love the sea that sets him free
and anchors me to the shore.

My Brother's Poem

I see the lost look in your eyes
    and hear in you despair;
the sunshine of the day belies
    the darkness everywhere.
As problems loom so large, so dense
    you cannot see the light,
you're filled with overwhelming sense
    of doom and hopeless fright.
The world, as seen from where you are,
    is masses of confusion;
and every word you hear of hope
    seems ignorant delusion.

Relax, my brother, be not afraid,
    for as your vision grows,
the dark you see becomes the shade –
    the sun forever glows.
We have a long, hard road ahead
    and seem sometimes as savage;
the earth still sees that we be fed,
    'though we plunder, waste and ravage.
Your sorrow now is like a knife –
    it butchers hopes and dreams.
Believe, my brother, in the power of life –
    It's stronger than it seems.

About the author

Susan Lannan Hicks lives in Waynesville, North Carolina, at the edge of the great Smoky Mountains.

After years of work in education and nonprofit services, both paid and volunteer, and of caring for and about friends and family members, she is ready to share some threads of understanding she gathered along the way.

For more information, visit susanhicks.info.

Acknowledgements

Cover design: Kimberly McClure, White Studios; www.whitestudios.us
Front Cover art by Joan Doyle: "Western North Carolina Dogwoods"
www.theartistryoflife.com
Back cover portraits and Peace Tree design by Kerra Hicks
Photograph on p. 22 was previously published in the Duquesne University literary magazine. Photographs at the bottom of p. 22 appear courtesy of the Wallace family. Author photo by Iron & Wax Photography. Other photos by Susan and Tom Hicks.
"To Oliver" was previously published in the Penn State University, Capital Campus, literary magazine.

Referred to in this volume:
Dr. Joseph F Arme, DC PA retired
Jane Barr, Executive Coach, PCC, ELI-MP, RIM; kinnexion.com
Orla Hazra, founding board member of Deeptime Network, dtnetwork.org

With many thanks to all of the above people who have contributed to creating this book and to all who have inspired me and encouraged me in my writing. Special thanks to my first reader, most ardent supporter, best friend and husband, Tom Hicks.

www.ingramcontent.com/pod-product-compliance
Lightning Source LLC
Chambersburg PA
CBHW051550010526
44118CB00022B/2654